THE SILENT KILLER

Breaking Free from Offense

Copyright© 2022 - Emily Strickland

This book or any portion thereof may not be reproduced or used in any manner whatsoever without the expressed or written permission of the author, except for the use of brief quotations in a book review or post.

Printed in the United States of America

Scripture quotations marked KJV are taken from the King James Version.

Scripture quotations marked NLT are taken from the Holy Bible, New Living Translation, copyright© 1996, 2004, 2207, 2013, 2015 by Tyndale House Foundation. Used by permission of Tyndale House Publishers, Inc., Carol Stream, Illinois 60188. All rights reserved.

"Scripture quotations are from the ESV® (The Holy Bible, English Standard Version®), copyright ©2001 by Crossway, a publishing ministry of Good News Publishers. Used by permission. All rights reserved."

Scripture quotations marked CEV are taken from the Holy Bible Common English Version. Copyright © 2011 by Common English Bible. All rights reserved.

"The Scripture quoted are from the NET Bible® http://netbible.com copyright © 1996, 2019 used with permission from Biblical Studies Press, L.L.C. All rights reserved".

Information on "Negative Bias" comes from the website skillpath.com.

Public domain

Please note that the author's style capitalizes certain pronouns that refer to the Father, Son, and Holy Spirit, and may differ from other writers' preferences and styles.

Scripture in bold and italicized by author for added emphasis.

All definitions come from Merriam-Webster dictionary.

First printing, 2022
Kindle Direct Publishing
ISBN: 9798370981333

THE SILENT KILLER

Breaking Free from Offense

Emily Strickland

Dedication

This book is dedicated to those who struggle with offense. This spirit is silent but deadly and if not dealt with, will kill off your spiritual walk. Offense is like weeds that just grow and choke the life out of everything else around it that is good and healthy. You must pull those weeds out of your garden, so you can become everything God intends for you to become.

Acknowledgements

First, I want to acknowledge Jesus. He is the lover of my soul and my very best friend. This book would not be possible without Him. Thank you for this gift, God. I pray I please you with my work.

Secondly, I want to acknowledge my husband Chaz. He is literally my greatest support and is the love of my life. Thank you for always listening to my book ideas and reading over my work for me. I appreciate you beyond words boo. I love you so much.

I also want to thank my four babies and the one that is on the way. It is because of you all that I have inspiration. You guys are my treasures. You are the stars in my sky. Without you all my life would have little meaning. Mommy loves you.

To my parents, mom in love, and brothers and sisters. I love and thank each one of you. May the blessings of God be upon you. May you all forever prosper.

To my church Ignite the Globe… you guys' rock! I love you all dearly. Thank you for allowing me front row seats into your walk with God. To say I am proud of you is an understatement. Keep burning for Jesus.

Chris Negron, thank you for your amazing covers. I love the work you always do for me. I appreciate you and you make it so easy to work with you. Thank you for your beautiful work and getting it done in a timely manner. You are the best.

To Acurracy4sure. You are a beast with formatting. Thank you for your hard work. You always do a great job and do it in such a quick turnaround time. I truly appreciate you.

Foreword

Offense is one of the devil's most powerful weapons. Offense can be connected to a person's immaturity and trauma, or it can be influenced by demonic activity in the spiritual realm. Jesus warned that because of offenses the love of many will wax cold. This is because offense directly impacts the spiritual condition of the heart. This is why when you meet a person who is bitter, angry, and full of unforgiveness and pride, there was always an incident that offended them at the root.

Offense is a door opener. There are countless believers who once had Gods supernatural fire in their life, that are spiritually sleeping, and the reason is some type of offense. The devil understands that new seasons, and even doors into destiny, can come in the form of a person. He wants to destroy these types of relationships because they are pregnant with potential. It is impossible to become all that you are called to be without people. Satan understands the role of parents, spiritual parents, spouses, mentors, and friends and he wants these types of relationships to be hindered by offenses leading us to carry dishonor and a disconnection from the blessings of these relationships.

My wife is more than qualified to write on this subject. In our thirteen years of marriage, I have learned so much about love through her. I was her first ministry assignment. God used my wife to help me unlearn unforgiveness and experience freedom from the spirit of offense and all the heart conditions written about in this book. It's one thing to preach a message but it's a whole other thing to embody your message.

In this book, my wife Emily is going to help equip you to overcome this subtle yet effective weapon of the enemy. This book carries wisdom for the reader to position themselves for inner healing and deliverance from trauma, rejection, and other bondages. Inside these pages you will discover keys and strategies that will protect the flame of God that lives in you, help you never lose a divine relationship, and as well walk in an unconditional love. Read and reread this book until you find freedom. My wife and I are rooting for you!

Chazdon Strickland

Author of: Supernatural Upgrade

Keys to Walking in the Glory Realm

Contents

Dedication v

Acknowledgements vii

Foreword ix

Introduction 1

Chapter 1 Misunderstandings and Perceptions 5

Chapter 2 Envy and Jealousy 17

Chapter 3 Guilt and Shame 27

Chapter 4 Insecurity and Low Self-Esteem 37

Chapter 5 Manipulation and Domination 47

Chapter 6 Unforgiveness and Bitterness 61

Chapter 7 Pride and Deception 71

Chapter 8 Immaturity and Rejection 81

Conclusion 91

A Call to Repentance 93

About the Author 95

Introduction

We have all dealt with offenses before. Offenses are something that come upon us easily, but we cannot stay there. It is not so much that you have been or even will be offended again at some point, the problem is when you stay in that offended place and make it your home. Offenses were meant to make us better, not become a dwelling place where we feel entitled to rest in that said offense. As growing people, we must do better.

There is a verse in Proverbs that talks about this very thing. It says at the end of the verse… ***And it is his glory to overlook an offense (Proverbs 19:11)***. What does that even mean you may be asking? God gets glory from everything we do when done in His ways and likeness. The Lord overlooks offenses all the time, so who are we that we cannot do the same?

I am not saying you will not feel the blow of the offense or be hurt by it. This also does not mean you overlook offense and pretend it never happened but what you do is get through it, talk it out, forgive, and ultimately choose not to become bitter because of it. We have no right to hold onto being wronged, when God has forgiven us of *much*. We must learn sooner than later to look beyond what is offending us and get

Introduction

to the nature of that offense within ourselves, so we can deal with the actual root of the problem. That is what I hope this book will help you achieve.

In this book I have outlined many of the characteristics that I have seen attach themselves to offense. In each chapter I outlined two major ones and then highlighted a lot of the small ones that branch off the main ones. Offense is a system in the enemy's arsenal of weapons to use against us. This is exactly why I want to bring these littles foxes to the light. They are deadly… Though small and if accepted, they will lead you to a life unfulfilled.

As you take this journey look within yourself and become delivered, so you can heal appropriately and completely. There is no reason to stay stuck in something that means you harm. You have a right to freedom, and I pray you take the opportunity. This is your chance to look within you and fight against this silent but deadly enemy. You have all the tools needed to beat this thing. Are you ready?

Take your time through this book. Read it more than once, because I have found that new things make themselves known to me when I reread something. Stay in the chapters that you really feel are hitting home and get delivered from that strong hold. Your growth in God is dependent on one real thing… YOU. I believe breakthrough and freedom go hand and hand, so allow God to breakthrough your offenses and set you free, because whom the Son sets free, is free indeed (John 8:36).

Chapter 1

Misunderstandings and Perceptions

Misunderstandings are going to happen. We are all different in our upbringing and backgrounds, so we communicate and behave differently. This is a good thing in the sense of us all not being identical. We want the world to be a unique and diverse place. Yet, certain things said certain ways can and will hurt people.

Here is an example. You say something to someone, and they misunderstand what you meant. The misunderstanding stems from either the delivery, what and why you said something, or from their own perceptions (I will talk about perceptions a little later in this chapter). For these very reasons misunderstanding can become so detrimental because it is a hard one to sometimes navigate. We must be patient with ourselves and one another in misunderstandings.

Misunderstandings and Perceptions

Okay, so let us take a moment to talk about delivery. There are people I know like myself, my husband, and especially people from up North that are very straight forward. For others who are not so straight forward, they can take they way one speaks and become offended by the delivery of something. How do we combat that you may be asking? Easy, we do our best as individuals to use caution when we speak and to work on ourselves to get to know someone by their heart, so that we can understand their delivery method.

Straight forwardness is not a bad thing, rudeness and abrasiveness are. I grew up in Ohio and was always taught to speak my mind and to be honest and blunt with people. Now, that does not mean I was raised to be disrespectful, rude and abrasive in my delivery and verbiage. There is a huge difference between the two. Anyone who feels that it is okay to be nasty in their exchange with people are absolutely wrong in that thought process.

Now, let me break down the second reason. What and why you are saying something to someone? We must be honest within ourselves, that there are times things do not even need to be said. One thing I have noticed, especially within the last ten years, is that people can be really mean. We think that everyone must be this said way or do things the way you may do it. Truth be told, that is not the case. There are many ways to do something and just because it is not your exact way, doesn't make it any less right.

We as people must learn to accept others for what they can bring to the table. Difference is not wrong and learning something a new way is not a bad thing. It is time for us to learn to embrace others and love them just the way they are. That does not mean that we cannot help them heal and grow and as we do that, we too can do the same. We are supposed to learn and grow from one another. The Bible says… ***iron sharpens iron… (Proverbs 27:17)***. It does not say that iron sharpens plastic, it is telling us that we are all made of iron and can make one another that much better.

The first thing you must do as a Christian is look inside yourself. Is God pleased with how you handled that misunderstanding? As the one being misunderstood is there possibly something you did to cause the misunderstanding? As the one who misunderstood, is there possibly something within you that is easily offended? After you do this what is the next step?

The next step is going to the person who you offended or whom you are offended with. If we could just follow the Biblical protocols that God has outlined within His word for us, we would be so much better as individuals and collectively. Here is what the Bible tells us. ***Moreover if thy brother shall trespass against thee, go and tell him his fault between thee and***

him alone: if he shall hear thee thou hast gained thy brother (Matthew 18:15 KJV). This is what God has asked of us, but how many of us actually do this?

As a leader in the body of Christ I can honestly say that I have seen offense play out many times. In nine out of the ten times I have witnessed it, it has never gone well. Many people do not go to the person, they just gossip to others about their offense. Most of the time the misunderstanding is something silly and could have been handled and moved past if the parties involved had just talked it out. It is sad to see things like that destroy great friendships and hinder churches.

Misunderstanding is defined as *a failure to understand something correctly.* As I said, this can be from both sides. It is time we realized that the enemy loves to make people misunderstand. It is sad to see many falling into this snare repeatedly. Wake up and see what the devil is doing in your life and stop letting him trap you.

I want to show you a Biblical story where Paul dealt with misunderstanding, and he handled it the correct way. We can learn a thing or two from it. Take the time even after reading about it here and go read it in the Bible. After reading it a few times. Expand on it and execute it in your own life and walk with Christ. We all can do better, and I do mean we *all* can.

I am not going to write the scripture verbatim, but I will give you the gist of what was going on. This misunderstanding is found in 2 Corinthians chapter 1. Here we see Paul writing a letter to the church of Corinth. As you read through the letter you will see that the people were upset with Apostle Paul. Why is the question at hand?

The misunderstanding stemmed from Paul saying he was coming to them at this specific time and then him changing his mind and going elsewhere first. They felt he was being fickle. Yet, that was never the truth at all. He did not just change his mind out of nowhere. It was something he felt the Lord led him to do.

Here is the scripture showing you exactly what I am saying. *And with this confidence I intended to come to you first so that you would get a second opportunity to see us, and through your help to go on into Macedonia and then from Macedonia to come back to you and be helped on our way into Judea by you, therefore when I was planning to do this, I did not do so without thinking about what I was doing, did I? Or do I make my plans according to mere human standards so that I would be saying both "Yes, yes" and "No, no" at the same time (2 Corinthians 1:15-17 NET)?* Here you see where Paul is confronting them in a kind but straightforward way about the misunderstanding. He is saying "Do you really believe that I would just change my mind without a cause and my yes, not be yes or my no, not be no?"

Apostle Paul continues in telling them that he is faithful in his meaning just as God is yes and Amen in

Misunderstandings and Perceptions

His promises. The true reason for the change of plans was to spare them. He had already corrected them for something else previously and did not want to pay them another painful visit. Not from fickleness, but because he hurt having to write them the first letter of correction. He wanted to come and bring them joy and feel happiness from them too.

This approach was the exact way Christ would have us handle misunderstanding. Paul's letter was full of love, hope for reconciliation, and yet, was straight to the point. If we did the same thing when something negative or not quite right was brought to our attention, we would see the body of Christ become much healthier. We handle misunderstandings so incorrectly and we as a *body* suffer because of it. People would not walk off and leave totally offended if those who were more mature confronted this nonsense and quickly but proficiently killed the seeds before they sprouted into full blown offense.

As I told you earlier, misunderstandings are bound to happen. You cannot control that part, but what you can control is how you handle it. You do not have to fly off the deep end if someone comes to you with an offense. People should not be afraid to come and share with you that they were hurt or offended by you with something you may have done or did not do. If you did not do something the way the person is saying, you can kindly explain that to the other party. No one should have to walk on eggshells around you.

On the other side of the coin, if you are offended by someone you should be a big enough person to go to them and them alone. Too many times I have seen back biting and gossip ensue because the person did not just do what the Bible asked. When we involve other people into something that is not their actual business, their advice could be very one sided and/or negative because they are seeing it from one point of view. This is why the Bible says go to the person straight way. We can and many of us have misunderstood things.

Just because there has been a misunderstanding, it does not mean that the misunderstanding cannot be reconciled. If you look at the word misunderstanding, you can literally break it down into two separate words. It means miss/understanding, so you missed the understanding. Even though you missed something once before, certainly does not prove that you cannot catch it next time around. You just must be willing to try again.

With a willingness to take another shot at it, there is a high chance that you will get it right this time around. And if nothing else, at least a lesson will be learned. You will know what not to do next time. We can become better from even the slightest of changes. This is a great reason to try and try again.

I am going to move off misunderstanding and go into perception now. I wanted to put them together because they go hand and hand. If you deal with one, you most likely deal with them both. You will need to be educated on both spirits and get deliverance from them together. Let's jump right in.

Perception is another way people are offended. As I stated earlier, perception is similar to misunderstanding, but a bit different. The definition of perception is *a way of regarding, understanding, or interpreting something*. So, where misunderstanding is a failure to see something, perception is your opinion of what you are seeing. Just because you see something one way, does that mean that it is truly that?

I cannot tell you how many times, (especially back when I was dealing with the issues within me), that I would see something one way only to find that it was completely different from what I interpreted. Many of us do this all the time. Maybe not purposefully, but we do it out of habit. We also can do it from a tainted lens within us. If everything in you stems from a negative connotation, I can guarantee you that what you perceive will also stem from a negative viewpoint.

This in and of itself makes it a problem for many. Until we are a new creation in Christ, we will continuously look through that warped lens at everything and everybody. When I hear someone saying that this person is dealing with this, and I saw this spirit in that one, etc. I am always on alert and find fault-finding and shaming as red flags, and what it highlights to me is that there is something off within you. Pointing the finger always leaves more fingers pointed back towards you.

Perceptions are important to have and can save you from harm and danger. Yet, when our surroundings are dysfunctional, our past experiences are not good, and our emotions are unbalanced, we can easily find our perceptions to lead us incorrectly. We must learn to recognize this up front and get the help we need to correct this. Then once healed we can use our perceptions as the driving force to our reactions to the things we see. It is a needed gift from the Lord, but it is a gift that must be blood washed and used with a renewed mindset.

The Bible even talks about how we keep on hearing, but do not understand. As well as that we keep on seeing, but do not perceive. This is paraphrased from Matthew 13:14. Who wants to be forever hearing, but never comprehending or forever seeing, but never perceiving? I want to have wisdom because the Bible even says in all thy getting, get understanding (Proverbs 4:7). I want to have spiritual perception, because I do not want to see incorrectly and lead myself and others astray.

I pray that you too will see how important it is to correct these things within you. For you to walk closer with God you must be willing to fix the things inside you even if they seem small and unnecessary to change. Small foxes are what spoil the fruit inside of us. Do not stop at just giving your life to Christ but pursue Him and become more like Him in *every* way. This is your opportunity to deal with you and truly find freedom.

Prayer

Father,

Thank You for showing me what it is that I am dealing with. I ask that You continue to highlight these things inside of me. I will not back down, but I will be willing to give everything up to become better and to ultimately be more like You. I want to be made in Your image and likeness. I want to be a reflection of You Abba.

I do not want misunderstanding or my own perceptions to mess up the new me that I have become. I desire more of You. I am going for the deeper, the more. I want to be lost in Your abyss and captured by Your beauty. I am giving You all of me.

No longer will I be comfortable in the ankle deep, the knee deep, nor the waist deep. I have decided to go all the way in. I am going into the ocean of You and getting lost in the depth of You. May Your deep always call out to my deep. May I always surrender to Your deepness.

These things must go now in Jesus's name. Dysfunction, misunderstanding, and perception go now. Leave me, leave my heart, leave my mind, right now. I want to walk in love and not my own opinions and feelings. Thank You Father for my deliverance.

In Jesus's name, Amen.

Chapter 2

Envy and Jealousy

My God today, I see these spirits in work way too often. I must be honest that I see it mostly within women. There are men who have it too and I am going to address it inside both women and men. Yet, it is prevalent inside women for a reason, and I will share that later in this chapter. These are very serious spirits that love to stir up offense. They linger inside of jealousy and envy and stir up very serious thoughts and feelings within people.

Envy can easily lead to jealousy if not dealt with swiftly. Many get these two words confused, or better yet they use them synonymously. They are actually quite different. Envy is defined as: *the painful feeling of wanting what someone else has, i.e., attributes or possessions.* An example would be you have been working your fingers to the bone all year, just dreaming of going on a vacation to Jamaica. After daydreaming of being on that beach just resting, you scroll Facebook and see one of your friends on the very vacation you just wished you were on. This may cause envy to rise inside of you.

Jealousy is not the same. The meaning of jealousy is feeling threatened, protective, or fearful of losing your position or situation to someone else. This alone can cause hostility to enter, which can then trigger action through anger or resentment. So, being envious can be a normal emotion that hits because you desire something, but if left undealt with can lead to jealousy which is far more damaging. Therefore, it is imperative that you deal with it upfront before it because stronger.

Both spirits will leave you with offense because they make you covet what belongs to another. When you want something, you may not be able to have, you can very quickly become offended. Offense then leaves you angry, resentful and eventually bitter. Bitterness can and will destroy you. The enemy's plan is always destruction.

We must always be willing to see these things for what they are and not just glaze over them like they are nothing. Every emotion we feel is not good nor helpful to our mind, body, or soul. Am I saying you cannot feel emotions, or even express yourself through your emotions? No, I am not saying that at all. You just should not be ruled by your emotions. Use them when needed, but do not let them use you. Emotions are not necessarily a bad thing at all, but when guided only by emotions you will certainly get into a lot of trouble.

Okay, let me take a minute to get into the women vs men thing with this envy/jealousy thing. Men deal with jealousy/envy because God created them with a dose of it within them. This is because of the protector that is inside them and as well because of the natural given pride that was placed in a man's DNA. They are not going to ever get all the way away from theirs because God strategically put in within them. They can steward it correctly though.

How you might be asking? Easy, with patience and some deliverance. Deliverance is the children's bread. If we eat that said bread, we can experience that needed deliverance. When patient we allow patience to have its perfect work in us. We truly need both when dealing with these types of spirits.

As I said men, you will not be able to remove these entirely because God placed this within your DNA to help you lead rightly. These same attributes are within God the Father as well. He gave you everything manly that is inside of His very nature. Use these attributes wisely because them being used within the realms of what God placed them there for, you will see much fruit created. When used from a negative place outside of God's nature you have tapped into something totally different that will lead you down a dark and lonely path.

Now women let me take a moment to share with you. We are as well created in the likeness of God. The difference is the attributes He gives both sexes. Where the male has the manly or firmer sides of Him. The Lord gives us the softer or better known to us as the womanlier side of things.

Once again this is not a bad thing for us either. God sovereignly chose to put it inside of us, so we could take care of our children. Children need their mothers to be nurturing and full of love to give them that softer part as well as the harder things from their father's. God created balance within the family unit for the interest of all parties. It is a beautiful mixture of all things God inside the family unit when done correctly.

This is why the enemy comes in to pervert the things God has placed within us each as a whole and individually. Women we must be mindful of calling our good evil and our evil good. It is not a good thing to be filled to the brim with jealousy and envy because it ruins our softer nature. Women are not supposed to be manly in any way, shape, or form. What do I mean by this?

I mean that women were made distinctly different than men. We are both unique in our natures and functions. As women we should be displaying the softer and gentler sides of Abba Father, where men will showcase God's masculinity. As a woman I will be faster to speak a soft answer, I will be more nurturing to my children and even my husband, this means hugging, cuddling, trying to heal what hurts, etc., I as well should be gentler in my approach to most things. Men are strong and quick to protect because of that strength, their discipline would be more seemingly aggressive, (not saying it is aggressive, but it stems from their strength and masculinity) where their correction would come out sharper and stronger, they as well will be quicker to probably show anger because of the nature that is within them.

For this very reason the enemy tries so hard to blur the lines of gender because if he can confuse us in our identities, he can destroy the family unit. Women we must fight against these things with fervency. This is exactly why it is not in our nature to be envious and jealous. Women are supposed to be more understanding and helpful. We were literally created as helpmeets in the first place.

I tell you until we get this thing right, we are always going to go wrong. We must see the devil for exactly what he is and stop falling for his shenanigans. He does it repeatedly and we continuously fall for his same dumb tricks. He has been pitting women against one another for so long and it is the same old sad story every time. When are we going to do better?

Look at the story of Leah and Rachel. It was a story laced with envy and jealousy and guess what those two spirits produced? You guessed it right… strife, murmuring, complaining, and gossip. This is the makeup of so many women now, that it is sickening. Angry, hateful, and just downright nasty.

The enemy has come hard against the Proverbs 31 woman. The sweet, tender, understanding, and confident woman is being erased. We are silently but swiftly being replaced with a demonic pseudo-woman. I plead for my ladies to get a realization of who you are and who God called you to be and walk in it boldly like Esther. Get like Ruth and be the woman of virtue that God created you to be. You will always be greater in your original design than anything else you could ever create for yourself.

I did not intend to go into that long tangent about women, but I really felt Holy Spirit impressing that truth within me to share with you beautiful ladies that are reading this book. We are more than our emotions and do not have to prove our strength through dominance and control. Be soft, be sweet and watch how you catch more bees with honey than vinegar. Your strength comes from the gentleness within you, your beauty speaks to the kindness that is you. Those attributes are magnificent, and God never creates things incorrectly. Embrace the you that He created you to be and simply soar through His truth.

The Bible even tells us this. Look at this scripture. *I will praise thee; for I am fearfully and wonderfully made: marvellous are thy works; and that my soul knoweth right well (Psalm 139:14 KJV).* As you see here, we are all fearfully and wonderfully made. Therefore, the fear of God was on display when He created us and He did it with precision and perfection, so we should have no second thoughts of who we are because of Him nor who we are inside of Him as His creations.

We as well should know that we know that we are amazing in our own unique designs. The scripture even says that our souls know it right well. That means we will always know deep in the core of ourselves who we are and who's we are. There is no getting away from the truth that He has lined up in the very fibers of our being. That is both man and woman, you may try to run from it, and/or hide from it but you will never be able to outrun truth.

Okay, back to the discussion at hand… Envy and jealousy. These two things, as are all these spirits that are attached to offense, which is dysfunction, are two that will ruin you exponentially. You will never find happiness in what God has given you. You will be disappointed time and time again. Until you deal with the root of the problem, which is envy and jealousy, you might as well count joy as a loss.

What happens if you don't is a pride that leads right into offense. I consider pride as disillusioned self-righteousness. You act like you think you are better, but you are really a pretender who knows that you are lacking. Having pride like this leads you into offense because it makes you believe you have the right to be mad at someone else. Yet, what right do you truly have to be mad?

This is delusion at its finest. You have no true reason to be angry at someone, yet you are. The only real reason you are mad is because they have something you do not. Make that make sense to me. I know you cannot, can you?

That is a reason within itself to correct the problem immediately. The Bible even tells us not to hate our brother without cause. Let's read this scripture together. *But I say unto you, That whosoever is angry with his brother without a cause shall be in danger of the judgement... (Matthew 5:22 KJV)*. When you are offended by someone, you are now in danger of being judged for that very thing.

God is a good Father. He is fair in His love and judgements. As we know, He is not a respecter of persons (Romans 2:11). This is His law; He is the law of His written word, and He does exactly as it states. Therefore, He will judge you for offense.

Take some time and do some deep introspection and see what God is showing you concerning this chapter. Are you dealing with envy, jealousy, strife, gossip, backbiting, etc.? If you are even to the slightest degree, handle that in prayer and be set free. Only being honest with yourself can bring you to that place of freedom. And trust me, there is nothing like freedom.

Prayer

Lord,

My goodness, this blessed me. I had no clue I was even dealing with these two things at all. I want to be free for real, so I ask that You make me free. I come humble before You and bow at Your feet. Set me free Jesus.

Envy and jealousy will not be a part of my makeup and identity. I will walk this thing out because I do not want to be hindered in my pursuit of You. I also do not want to stop progressing in my becoming more like You. Therefore, I ask You to highlight these things when they rear their ugly heads and remove them out of my life for good. I want You and You alone.

Thank You for loving me enough to show me this truth. Thank You for revealing these things to me so I can be better. I am working to get free from offense and all that comes with it. Every demon attached to this silent killer must go. I will be completely free in Jesus' name, Amen.

Chapter 3

Guilt and Shame

I remember dealing with these spirits extremely bad before I met Jesus and got free. These are two spirits that are very crippling. They can really destroy your life, to the point of not only self-condemnation but depression and suicide. Guilt and shame work hand and hand, but they are different. The end result is always negative and settles you in offense.

The thing is, when I say offense, I mean deep offense to the point of not only being offended with others, but even being offended with yourself. Guilt and shame always reflect you to yourself and make you condemn yourself to the point of self-hatred and/or self-harm. They are spirits that attack you more than others. You may try to blame others, or be angry towards other people, but these two's main objective is to cause you to blame and be angry at yourself. They are here to destroy YOU first and foremost.

Let me jump right in and share with you some of the affects of these detrimental spirits. My hope is that when you read through them, you can get a better

Guilt and Shame

picture of why you want to be free from them. You do not have to carry these demons around with you. You are not called to live in guilt and shame for the rest of your life. Let's get free today.

Okay, so first what are guilt and shame? Guilt is a feeling you get when you did something wrong or think that you might have done something wrong. Shame is where you feel ashamed, humiliated, or distressed inside of yourself because of wrong or foolish behavior. Shame makes you feel like you as an individual are wrong. Where guilt makes you feel you need to right the wrong you committed.

So, as we see, guilt can usually lead you to redemption, where shame usually leads you to unredeemable regret. Regret is not always a bad thing, but it can be if it is toxic regret. Shame usually causes toxic regret. Toxic regret is the type of regret that you are not worthy of forgiveness or what you did wrong was so bad that there is no coming back or making up for that offense. This is the type of regret that leads to depression and/or suicide.

There is a story in the Bible that I am going to point out here to show you exactly the type of deep-seated shame I am talking about. It is a sad story. One that could have gone a different way if the regret would have been from guilt and not from shame. Are you ready to hear it? Let's go.

This is the part of the Bible where Judas betrayed Jesus. Judas was one of Jesus's twelve disciples. This means that he was called to walk closer to Jesus than other's who only followed from afar. He was one of the men chosen to be a disciple of Jesus. This is why it is quite funny to me, that he did not reverence Jesus in the same way the other disciples did.

If you walked with Jesus while he was here on earth and witnessed Him do the miracles, signs, and wonders that He did what name would you call Him? I know for me personally it would not have just been Rabbi. I would have witnessed enough things to know within myself that He was the Messiah. Therefore, His name to me would have been Lord. All the other disciples called Jesus Lord, but Judas only called Him Rabbi.

This means that Judas *only* saw Him as just another teacher and nothing more. Which indicates to me that Judas probably did not have a deeper revelation of Jesus being the Savior. He never saw Jesus for who He truly was, so that in turn would make it a lot easier to betray someone who you never really reverenced nor recognized. Not only did Judas disrespect Jesus in His true nature, but he also was full of greed. His being greedy as well added to the fact of his selling Jesus out for thirty pieces of silver.

Let's read on from that point. ***Then saith one of his disciples, Judas Iscariot, Simon's son, which should betray*** *him, why was not this ointment sold for three hundred pence, and given to the poor? This he said, not that he cared for the poor; but because he was a thief, and had the bag, and bare what was put therein (John 12:4-6 KJV)*. Did you read that? As we can see Judas showed us one, that he did not even believe that Jesus was worthy of having precious oil poured out upon Him and two, that he wanted the money to take of it as he desired to.

Now, let me jump to what happened after he sold Jesus out. This is the important part that brings us to the guilt and shame. *Then Judas, which had betrayed him, when he saw that he was condemned, repented himself, and brought again the thirty pieces of silver to the chief priests and elders, saying, I have sinned in that I have betrayed the innocent blood. And they said, What is that to us? See thou to that. And he cast down the pieces of silver in the temple, and departed, and went and hanged himself (Matthew 27:3-5 KJV)*.

Here is what stands out and reveals that he not only had guilt, but he had shame also. When Judas saw that Jesus was condemned, he repented within himself. This showcases that he felt guilty because guilt usually brings about repentance, that then brings you to redemption. The problem is, he did not only feel guilty, but he felt shame because he turned it inward and believed he was unredeemable. Let's look at how this is so.

The Silent Killer

Verse three goes on to tell us that he repented himself and then he takes the silver back. He was hoping for redemption through those two actions. Yet, what greeted him was the priests saying "what is this to us, meaning why come back now? This end result of Jesus being condemned is what we wanted the entire time, and we where able to buy you to do it." After that interaction with them is when Judas became so deeply ashamed that he felt he himself was unforgivable and beyond repair. What happens next is what shame always tries to bring you to, suicide. We see this in verse five, where he cast down the pieces of silver in the temple, left, and went and hanged himself.

He hanged himself because he had zero hope for this outcome becoming different, he regretted what he did, and he was so ashamed that he could only repent within himself. He tried to right the wrong by giving the money back, but he never went and repented to the one he actually did the wrong to. This is how shame works; it fills you with so much condemnation that hope becomes differed and you feel useless and alone. Those are two of the characteristics connected to shame, uselessness and loneliness. They attach onto you quickly too.

The other problem here is that Judas already had offense in his heart towards Jesus. As I wrote up above, he felt that Jesus was unworthy to have the precious oil poured out on His feet. He as well did not see Jesus as the Messiah and disrespected Him by only calling Him Rabbi. Judas to some degree was offended with Jesus. I am not sure what it all the way stemmed from, but it was there subtly inside his heart. Therefore, when regret did hit him, he still could not go apologize and repent to Jesus. Whenever you have an offense within yourself towards another it makes it extremely difficult to do right by them.

I want to share some of the characteristics of guilt and shame as well. I want you to be able to identify what they are at any moment. Then if you see any of these within yourself you can adjust and get the deliverance you need. You do not have to carry around baggage that is unnecessary. Jesus came that the captives may be free. It is time that you become free.

Guilt and shame are heavy hitters with offense because the offense like with Judas is usually subtle, but still very present. Here are some of the characteristics that align with these spirits. Offense, jealousy, loneliness, anger, resentment, uselessness, depression, and suicide. I am sure there are more, but these are the ones coming to my mind right now. If you notice any of these or down the line ever notice any of them, go to God in prayer and seek deliverance.

People who usually deal with these spirits tend to have gone through some kind of trauma in their early years. We are all born with emotions, but some things are learned in many ways. If your emotions were shaped by dysfunction, you better believe it will be shown in everything you say and do. For example, if you were abused in your childhood and just blamed for everything and then beat for things you did and things you did not even do, I can guarantee you that you will feel guilty all the time for almost everything. This was a behavior that was shaped in you by trauma and abuse.

So many of these things are not our fault at all. We never want to be mistreated or brought to a place of negativity. Yet, we are products of our environments. This is why it is so important to gain healthy thinking, and habits as you grow. You do not have to stay the way you first were shown. You can make the choice to change and become better. This is the first step.

Guilt and shame takes hold of our self-image. That is why these demons work so hard at altering who you truly are because if they can get you in their grip, they can destroy you indefinitely. Entertaining these spirits for long periods of time causes them to bring about low self-esteem and eventually cause you to have no self-worth. Without having self-worth, you could not care less about you or anyone or anything else. This is one way these spirits lead you into depression.

True guilt is not a bad thing because guilt helps you do what is right and go and apologize. It is a good thing to feel convicted. God is bothering your conscience and causing you to feel regret for an incorrect behavior. That is a beautiful and courageous thing when moved on appropriately. I see no problem in this type of guilt.

The problem lies in the person who sees guilt through the lens of negativity. This is when guilt can become shame. Once shame gets inside you, you have gone from conviction to condemnation and now you feel damaged beyond repair. This thought process is unhealthy and will keep you from moving into deeper relationships with people because your view of everyone will be tainted. Offense will become your defense mechanism. For this reason, you must be freed from these spirits.

I hope this chapter helped you see why and how offense lurks in so many different emotions. I know it is easy to assume that guilt and shame would have nothing to do with offense, but offense is so much deeper than we could even imagine. It has been rearing its ugly head for so long and I see a very little amount of people calling it out. Yet, I see so many lives being ruined by it's death bite repeatedly. I am praying you are breaking out of its grasp as you read.

Prayer

Lord,

Wow, these are some real spirits that are literally trying to take me out of here. I ask for Your protection over my life Father. Help me to see the truth inside of myself, so I do not keep falling into this same trap. Break me out of this funk and give me untainted vision. Help me to see even when I do not readily choose to.

I now understand that everything is not my fault. I am a human, and we all make mistakes. Your word even says that we all have fallen short of the glory. I know choose to see this as a steppingstone to do better. I am breaking out of these cycles of abuse and becoming a new creation.

Thank You for loving me enough to show me myself. I am not forever guilty; I am not ashamed to the point of brokenness. I am somebody. I can do better. I will choose me for You today and walk in my freedom. In Jesus's name, Amen.

Chapter 4

Insecurity and Low Self-Esteem

I wrote these two spirits together because they always go hand and hand. You will not find one without the other. Demons like to link up into pairs. When one comes along, it always brings company. Let's dive into this chapter and get informed, so we can get free.

I also dealt heavily with these two spirits. Boy, they almost took me out of here. I had to fight, and I mean fight for my life. They are two of the most crippling spirits I know to date. If not checked, these spirits will grow like weeds and cause your life to spin out of control.

I became a prisoner within myself. I mean locked up behind bars of self-hatred, victimization, and offense. These are just three of the tactics we fall victim to when we have these two spirits attached to us. It was horrible walking through life like that. A living, walking, and breathing zombie.

Insecurity and Low Self-Esteem

I will talk a little bit about insecurity, low self-esteem, self-hatred, victim mentality, and how they work to make you offended. *Insecurity is a feeling of uncertainty or anxiety, and lack of confidence in oneself. Low self-esteem is a negative perception one has about oneself.* When you have low self-esteem insecurity is always one of its characteristics. Perceiving yourself in any other way, but how Abba Father sees you is a recipe for disaster, and it causes so much damage to you.

Insecurity happens to the best of us. We could maybe be trying something new and feel some fear or uncertainty in our abilities, and that is normal. It is when we perceive negativity about us as an individual that we get into trouble. This goes beyond just feelings now. That is internalizing and looking at ourselves as uncertainty.

Self-hatred is now highlighted from having low self-esteem. This happens because we perceive ourselves in a negative light. *Self-hatred is intense dislike of oneself.* So, as you see you go from a negative perception of yourself, to intense dislike of yourself. This is how the devil always works, he does everything in levels.

Then there is having a victim mentality. This was something I did all the time. When you have low self-esteem, you tend to make yourself into a victim. Everything is someone else's fault, bad things will always happen, and I will never be able to stop or change them. This was how I always felt when I was dealing with this spirit.

I blamed everyone for everything. I never took responsibility for my own actions; I made excuses for my poor decisions. I was pessimistic in my thought process because bad things were always happening to me. What I did not realize was that I was giving off negativity, so negative things were always attracted to me. Our thoughts determine our life because we tend to act out the things we think.

This was my mind set for years on end. I let myself destroy any hope of a brighter future. I didn't even believe it was possible. Having a victim mindset is like being in a mental prison. The only thing is you are the prisoner, the warden, and the judge. You lock yourself away so tight, you throw away the key, and you become accustomed to the system. A system you created within yourself, and you live in self-pity, offense, and low self-esteem. And by the way, it is such a horrible way to live.

How does insecurity and low self-esteem lead to offense you are probably wondering? It starts with insecurity in the first place. Offense is defined as: *annoyance or resentment brought about by a perceived insult to or disregard for oneself or one's standards or principles.* This very definition is why it is so easy to take offense when you have insecurity and low self-esteem. As you see in the definition it says disregard for oneself. When you already feel disregard for yourself, what someone else says triggers things inside of you.

Here is the funny thing, having insecurity and low self-esteem causes many people to carry pride as well. It is crazy because you try hard to make other's see you in a light that you do not even see yourself in. That is why so many people who struggle with these two main spirits are so prideful and easily offended. It goes like this inside a person who is full of low self-esteem. "I am pretending to think I am better than what you just insulted me with, but I actually feel exactly what you said, but I am mad because how dare you see through my smoke and mirrors and then have the audacity to speak on the truth of what you really see in me".

This is the constant battle of thoughts in someone's head who suffers from these spirits. It is not any way to live because you easily play the victim, even when someone is trying to help you in love. You cannot see clearly, hear clearly, nor feel correctly because everything within you is full of so much negativity. It is a battle within yourself and outside of yourself all at the same time. You are literally fighting your whole self constantly.

That is why it is so hard to break out of low self-esteem. You have been beating yourself up so much that you have normalized the chaos and dysfunction within you. It is different trying to break out of mental bondage when it is your own cage that you put yourself in. It's one thing to break through a stigma that someone else placed on you, but it is a whole other thing when you must break through your own disgraces that you placed on yourself. It is not as easy to change your own mindset about you.

Yet, the good news is it can be done. Bringing about change for this one is a daily endeavor. Since you are dealing with inward dislikes, you must focus on outward strengths. What do I mean by this, you are asking? The Bible says *I lift up my eyes to the hills. From where does my help come? My help comes from the Lord, who made heaven and earth (Psalm 121:1-2 KJV).*

Your help will come from Jesus. When you put your focus on Him, He will begin to change you in the secret place. When you are learning how to love yourself, learning to love your creator will bring you to knowing how marvelous He finds His creation. In understanding this, after a while you will begin to believe and feel this same love for yourself. Transformation happens from a renewed mind set and the only way to gain one, is to not focus on fixing yourself.

Many think they can fix themselves. Trust me, I tell you this from experience. I tried to do it for many years. I would start off by saying "I'm going to turn over a new leaf." Yet, every new leaf I tried to find would eventually die and fall off my tree of good intentions like dying leaves falling to the ground in Autumn.

It took me longer than necessary to realize that I could not transform in and through my own strength. I had to use the strength of God, which is made to be perfect in my weakness (2 Corinthians 12:9). Jesus is the only one who is perfect, and He can pull me out of the areas I am weak in. I had to allow Him to do it by fully surrendering to Him and to His ways. When I gave Him all of me, got deliverance, and truly choose to walk it out is when though temptations came, they no longer could overtake me because I chose Jesus over them every time.

Insecurity and low self-esteem can only stay with you if you come into agreement with them. When you decide to say enough is enough and pursue God, He will pursue you and in doing that transformation has to take place. Nothing can really be in true relationship with Jesus and not actually change. It's impossible. He gives us life… meaning in Him is our purpose and being in purpose is our best life.

The thief comes only to steal and kill and destroy. I came that they may have life and have it abundantly (John 10:10 KJV). Abundant life is the Zoe kind of life. That is a life in and purposed through Christ Jesus. There is no other kind of life.

As you see in the scripture I just wrote, there are two different ways to live. One is true life and the other is not living at all and will only lead to destruction, darkness, and death. Many have chosen the latter. Maybe not intentionally, but your choices are leading you down a dark path. Jesus says this... *Enter by the narrow gate. For the gate is wide and the way is easy that leads to destruction, and those who enter by it are many. For the gate is narrow and the way is hard that leads to life, and those who find it are few (Matthew 7:13-14 KJV).*

There it is in a nutshell. It is a choice. What are you going to choose from this day forward? Are you going to chose to agree with these spirits or are you going to choose the one who came to save you? Offense wants you to make the wrong decision, remember, it is fueled by good intentions.

Okay, now after getting an understanding on all that, the final question is... How do insecurity and low self-esteem connect to offense? Easy! Those two spirits are breeding grounds for making offense settle in. I know because I dealt with them, and I would get offended so easily. Offense loves to live off these bad boys.

Let me speak on the victim mentality I talked about earlier. Being a victim of everything really leaves you quite vulnerable to satan's devices. Having a victim mentality is an open door for offense. The reason being is acting like a victim takes a lot of manipulation, (I will talk more about this in the next chapter) and depending on if your tactic of manipulation works or does not work determines if

Insecurity and Low Self-Esteem

offense snares you or not. Trust me more times than not, it will get ahold of you too.

Let me give you an example. I do something wrong, where it is clearly my fault and I blame someone or something else. I do not own up to the wrong I did, and simply make an excuse for my behavior. "I did it because I was hurt by so and so. If they would not have done what they did, I would not have done what I did." Then I get all sad and pouty or mad and dismissive. What happens next on your end will be what determines how the victim minded person responds.

Okay, so let's say you accept my poor behavior, either you really believe me, or you are pacifying me to shut me up. Either way, I won in the end, and I was able to manipulate you and the situation to get my way. Now, on the other hand let's say you do not accept my horrible behavior. You may be at the point called sick of it or you simply do not believe me. At this time, you expect me to own up to the wrong I did. I will now become mad and offended because I was not able to manipulate the situation. This scenario will eventually happen because people can only be tricked for so long before they become sick of someone's shenanigans.

This is just one way offense can settle in. There are many others because as I said earlier insecurity and low self-esteem is an easy opening for the enemy. You must fight against these spirits and let God have His way in your life. Insecurity and low self-esteem do not have to be your portions. You can come out of this, but you must be willing to do it the way God chooses. God set me free, I had to fight for my life, but anything worth having is worth fighting for. So, fight!

Prayer

Father,

I thank You for showing me this truth. I have been dealing with these demons long enough. I hate feeling this way towards myself and I want to be free. Today is my day of emancipation. I am going to walk right out of this place of darkness directly into Your marvelous light.

So here am I. I give myself to You. I am no longer going to try to do this my way because my way leads me further away from Your glory. It takes me further off course every single time that I try to do it on my own. I surrender my life to You oh God. Have Your way.

Insecurity and low self-esteem will no longer have their way in me. I no longer come into agreement with these devils. I rise above self- hatred, and I come out of negative thoughts and perceptions of myself. I speak that I am more than what I can equate. I am exactly who You say I am Lord. Thank You for loving me and helping me. In Jesus's name, Amen.

Chapter 5

Manipulation and Domination

These two run right over from our last chapter. Manipulation and domination are two that are activated through witchcraft of the flesh. This happens often when offense has entered your heart. You would not want to manipulate or dominate someone unless you feel threatened or entitled to some degree. We are going to get into it all right now.

Many think that manipulation just happens. I am here to tell you that this is not the case. Manipulation is a well-oiled action. It is a skill set to be honest. Even the definition says this. *Manipulation: The action of manipulating something in a skillful manner.* It takes skill to manipulate.

Domination is the direct action after manipulation. If you can manipulate someone, you certainly will begin to dominate them because you know you can. If someone gives you an inch, you take a mile. *Domination: The exercise of control or influence over someone or something, or the state of being so controlled.* So, you are exercising control over someone or a situation.

These two spirits work in tandem with each other. If you see one, I guarantee you will see the other. Once someone decides to manipulate, they have also chosen to dominate that relationship as well. These spirits work in scheming, lying, hiding, using, influencing, commanding, etc. They are sneaky and very persuasive.

Many who are overtaken by these spirits move in these actions first, maybe unknowingly. Yet, once they get a good thing going, they begin to like what they are getting out of it and begin to become comfortable in that one-sided relationship. They will then use the person up until there is nothing left to gain. Once the person is depleted the manipulator and dominator will move on to the next person. Allowing these spirits to have residence within you will cause you to walk down a continual path of vicious cycles.

These cycles will be on repeat and have you manipulated and dominated by them. You will think you are winning and all you are really doing is living a life that is not yours. You are living on borrowed time. Never having anything that is your own, that you have worked for will have you eventually feeling unsatisfied. The problem is then that you are so used to manipulating that you will struggle to disconnect from it all. Yet, in feeling unsatisfied and unfulfilled will then have you playing make believe with your life, which will keep you unfortunately soul tied to these two spirits.

I hear many of you saying, "I do not manipulate anyone". Well, let me ask you this, are you sure? Manipulation does not always look the same. It has different forms. There is outright manipulation, but there is also subtle manipulation.

Let me share some different ways you can manipulate someone. It could be out of pure need. You are struggling in life. Maybe you just do not have a lot and need something, so you just reach out to borrow a little bit. It really may be as simple as that but depending on how you are can cause it to lead to something more.

For example, if you are naturally an independent person, you just may be in need of something this one time around. On the flip side though, let's say you have a dependent personality and you have relied on people your entire life to take care of you, now we are seeing a monster being created. You are used to doing this and this is now not just a moment of need but a whole habit. Doing this can truly become you. That is why these spirits can be so dangerous.

So, let's say you are one who is not subtle with it anymore and it's just become a part of your makeup now. You have become so accustomed to having your way that you no longer even try to hide the sleight of your hand. You manipulate and dominate your husband or wife. You guys have been married for years and years now and you did not start off this way, but you have been hurt by them, so now you use that mistake to your advantage. You now demand them to live by your beacon call.

I have seen this many times in marriages that my husband and I have counseled. One spouse is upset with the other and says they have forgiven their spouse but by this behavior you can see that they have not forgiven them at all. They are trying to make them pay for something that they sadly will never be able to pay for. It is like saying… "You hurt me, so you will live to make me happy for the rest of your days." This is a horrible way to think and behave and will only leave both parties unhappy.

Marriage is not one sided. As a married person myself, I can understand the pain of being hurt by the person you would least expect it from. Yet, we must remember we too have probably hurt them before as well. Marriage is the place you learn to forgive the most because love is constant, but with love comes risk, and you vowed to love them for better or worse, richer or poorer, until death do you part. (Now, I do want to say that I am writing this to the point of certain things, no one deserves to be abused in any way, so make sure you are staying through normal situations). We cannot just mistreat our spouse because we are not happy with them.

The Silent Killer

Let me give you another example. This time you are the one being manipulated. Kids try to do this to their parents all the time. This is why it is very important you teach your kids to grow into well-behaved, responsible adults. If they are taught that they can have whatever they want, whenever they want it, you are highly likely to be leading them down a road of destruction. Spoiled kids usually become bratty adults, undisciplined children, normally become unlawful grownups.

There is always an exception to this, but I have seen it more times than once. I tell my kids no sometimes just to switch it up a little bit. My children as well have chores and expectations in their schooling to have the extra not necessarily needed things that they just want. Do they do what I want every time I ask? Absolutely not, but I see the responsibility and sensibility that is being developed within them because of how my husband and I raise them.

Okay, here is the example. You maybe were young when you had your kids, and it was just you that raised them. You did the best you could with the skillset and example you were given. It's possible you made tons of mistakes, (as all parents do let me add) your kids grow up and try to then use the harder times as a scapegoat for their behavior. You fall for it because you felt like you failed them in the past.

Let me say this is manipulation and domination at its finest. It is not okay to be held responsible for a grown person's behavior. I do not care if you were the worst parent on the planet. You apologize to them, forgive yourself, and then guess what you do? You release them. It is their choice to now decide if they want to get better or stay bitter.

You do not owe them anything. You can be there for them of course because you are their parent, and they will be for always and forever your child. There is a huge difference between being there for them and enabling them. If allowed to, they will use this excuse to manipulate you and dominate the situation for as long as they can abuse it. You must see it for exactly the demonic influence that it is and finally stand up for yourself.

These are just two different examples, but they are very common ones. Look at your own life and see if you too are either manipulating or being manipulated. If you see these things in your own life, please correct it because it is detrimental to you and all those who are around you. You can choose to change; you can as well say enough is enough and stop allowing someone to abuse you. It is all up to you my dear.

Now, I want to talk a little about the witchcraft part. These spirits are very active in the demonic, they thrive through using witchcraft. This is the key to their functioning within a person. Let's get into it. Are you ready?

The Silent Killer

The main things in witchcraft are manipulation, control, and then domination. Many who operate in witchcraft use its means to intimidate and manipulate. Their end game is to always control and dominate the person they are aiming to use.

Witchcraft is the manipulation of the flesh. It is easy to use as a tool because many are pulled by fleshly things. The enemy always paints this with a pretty red ribbon tied up on golden packages. He presents it to you through either the lust of the flesh, the lust of the eyes, and the pride of life (Read 1 John 2:15-16). That is why this is such a heavy hitter, because it incorporates all three things God ask us to be very careful of and causes you to love the world more than you love the things of God.

A great example of this spirit in action is Jezebel. Who is Jezebel? She was the daughter of Ethbaal, king of Sidon, the wife of the king of Israel, king Ahab, making her the queen of Israel. She advocated for the worship of false gods and was highly known for harassing and killing God's prophets. This woman was vile and full of witchcraft. Let's get right into it.

The first thing that must be noted is that Jezebel came from a lineage of witchcraft. Her father Ethbaal was noted to have been a priest of Astarte, which is the Greek name for the moon goddess Ashtoreth. He was frequently associated with the name Baal, which if you notice is the end of his own name Eth-*baal*. This tells us that she was very much groomed to be a high-ranking witch from the start. Ahab and Ethbaal were politically connected, which makes a probable reason as to why Ahab and Jezebel were married in the first place.

Their union at least to God was an even worse thing then the fact that king Ahab did more things to displease the Lord than any other king before him. Let me prove this to you. *Ahab did more things to disobey the Lord than any king before him. He acted like Jeroboam. Even worse, he married Jezebel the daughter of King Ethbaal of Sidon and started worshipping Baal (1 Kings 16:30-31 CEV).* Right there in verse 31 it says **even worse**, so it was not enough to just already disobey God, but you went beyond that and married the evil and vile Jezebel, who then brought strange gods to the Lord's chosen people for them to start worshipping, instead of continuing their worship to the one true and living God.

Israel before that had never worshipped any other god. Jezebel's first line of demonic agenda was to introduce false gods to Israel. She persuaded her husband to promote the worship of deities because that is what she was used to doing and was able to use manipulation to get her way. As we see in 1 Kings 16:32 Ahab builds an altar and a temple for baal in Samaria. He also set up a sacred pole for worshipping the goddess of Asherah.

The first thing she did was full of manipulation, as you see she persuaded her husband. Persuasion is a part of manipulation. You would think that would be enough because bringing false gods into a holy land is enough to disturb the entire balance of what was normal. That was not the end of her demonic agenda. Oh no, there is much more. As I told you earlier, it starts off with manipulation and then ends with control and domination.

Okay, let's jump to the next part. As you read on in 1 Kings you will come to the part where Jezebel has a man killed because he would not sell his vineyard to Ahab. The man's name is Naboth, and he owned a vineyard in Jezreel. One day Ahab said, "Naboth, your vineyard is near my house, let me have it so I can turn it into a garden. I can give you a better garden or pay you for that one."

Naboth declines this offer because this land was given to him as an inheritance from his father. Of course, the spoiled king Ahab is not happy because how dare anyone tell him no. He goes home angry and depressed to the point he will not even eat his food and just lays on his bed sulking. His wife Jezebel comes in inquiring what the matter is. He tells her that he wanted Naboth's vineyard, and he would not give it to him. What do you think she does?

You guessed it, she takes matters into her own hands. Listen to this manipulation and control. ***"Are you the king of Israel or not?" Jezebel demanded. "Get up***

Manipulation and Domination

and eat something, and don't worry about it. I'll get you Naboth's vineyard" (1 Kings 21:7 NLT)! Did you hear that not only did she demand him to get up, but she controlled the situation and then ended with domination by telling him she would get him Naboth's vineyard.

After this she continues with her manipulation, control, and domination by writing letters in her husband's name, sealing them with his seal, and then sent them to the elders and other leaders of the town where Naboth lived. In those letters she commanded the citizens together for a time of fasting, told them to give Naboth a place of honor, and to seat two scoundrels across from him who will accuse him of cursing God and the king, and then after they accuse him to take Naboth outside and stone him to death. The leaders of the town followed Jezebel's instructions and sent word back that they have killed Naboth. Here is what the Bible then says… **When Jezebel heard the news, she said to Ahab, "You know the vineyard Naboth wouldn't sell you? Well, you can have it now! He's dead!" So Ahab immediately went down to the vineyard of Naboth to claim it (1 Kings 21:15-16 NLT).**

My goodness how vile can you be? She couldn't care less that she killed an innocent man just so her husband could have what he wanted. That is manipulation and domination if I have ever seen it. The crazy thing is Ahab pretty much knew what she was going to do and certainly had no reservations about what she did because it said after she told Ahab that he could have it because Naboth was dead, that he *immediately* went down to claim Naboth's vineyard. So, not only did they kill Naboth, but they were also going to rob the man too. What they did was extremely evil and quite manipulative.

Eventually, God dealt severely with Jezebel. Therefore, she did not get away with the demonic agenda she pushed. The crazy thing is she died still trying to use her witchcraft called manipulation. Check this out. In 2 Kings, it shows her trying to tempt Jehu with her beauty. *Jehu approached Jezreel. When Jezebel heard the news, she put on some eye liner, fixed up her hair, and leaned out of the window (2 Kings 9:30 NET).*

She was hoping for Jehu to notice her beauty and then seduce him. Who really knows what she would have done to him if she had succeeded in manipulating him. In the end her tactic did not work, and he killed her. This is always the result of manipulation and domination. It may work for a time, but in the end, God deals with it all.

Reading on Jezebel should have you checking and double checking to be sure you are not moving in witchcraft of the flesh. I am telling you now that manipulation and domination *always* will lead to you opening yourself up to the spirit of Jezebel. Who wants to fall into that type of rebellion produced by satan? *For rebellion is as the sin of witchcraft, and stubbornness is as iniquity and idolatry (1 Samuel 15:23 KJV)*. Get free today!

Prayer

Lord,

Wow! I had no idea that was all connected. I do not want to work in witchcraft of any kind. Please deliver me from the desires of my flesh. Let me be more in tune with You to make my spirit man stronger.

I only want to move through You Holy Spirit. Allow me to repent right now on behalf of myself and my blood line. Forgive my forefathers of any alignment with satan. I ask forgiveness for any working of witchcraft. I repent right now and ask that my bloodline be washed clean in the name of Jesus.

Cover me in Your blood Lord and make me new. Mark me as Yours and call me son/daughter. I will not align myself with evil, nor open any door to the spirit of Jezebel. Save me from myself and set me free. I love You, Abba. In Jesus name I pray, Amen.

Chapter 6

Unforgiveness and Bitterness

I am excited to get into this chapter! The reason being is I see so many people in the Kingdom suffer with these two spirits. It is heartbreaking to witness. Being oppressed by these spirits ruins your life both spiritually and naturally. Okay, let's jump right on in.

We as Christians are called to forgive much and repeatedly. *Then came Peter to him, and said, Lord, how oft shall my brother sin against me, and I forgive him? Till seven times? Jesus saith unto him, I say not unto thee, until seven times: but, until seventy times seven (Matthew 18:21-22 KJV)*. I can hear you now oh that is not forever, I can forgive a few times or so. Yet, you are not supposed to read that scripture literally, but it should be read symbolically. Meaning read it as the never-ending way that we as children of God are called to forgive.

Forgiving is not always easy. Trust me, I know this from real life experiences. I was raped at gun point

Unforgiveness and Bitterness

at fifteen years old. That was bad all by itself, but to make matters worse, I was set up by a very close friend to be raped just so she could date my rapist. How absurd and evil is that?

So, I not only had to forgive the rapist that I barely knew, but I had to forgive someone who did me dirty that I called a friend. This was extremely hard, and I will tell you the truth, it did not happen overnight. That great news is this does not have to be your portion at all. The first problem in my journey to forgiveness was I was not a born-again believer. I was unable to see this from the heart of the Father because I did not have His heart to begin with.

The second issue is you cannot forgive someone for something when you do not realize you yourself have been forgiven of much as well. I am going to get into both of these problems as we continue in this chapter. We are going to get free from these spirits today. Unforgiveness has held you back long enough. Bitterness is not going to find a way to latch on to your heart.

Thirdly, you must want to forgive. This means not only are you forgiving the person who wronged you, but you are forgiving yourself for the wrong you have done. I am here to bring this truth to the forefront and help you to see the lies of the enemy. You will be free after this. Today is your day!

The Silent Killer

Okay, so let's deal with the first issue at hand. Not being reborn of the bloodline of Jesus Christ. Without doing this is not only going to be almost impossible to forgive, but you are not going to understand forgiveness to even be able to give it. Forgiveness is a root issue and years, and years of trauma can cause a lingering effect of hurt and anger and forgiveness will be the last thing on your mind. You must give your life to Christ first and foremost.

After being born again or if you already are a born-again believer, now it's time to learn the heart of the Father. Abba's heart is love above everything. *And now these three remain: faith, hope, and love. But the greatest of these is love (1 Corinthians 13:13 NET).* So, above everything is love. It is so very important to love despite the hard trials and the hurt that is so often caused by people.

Love is a freeing agent. It is beautiful to love no matter what because it keeps you out of bondage. It causes you not to become a slave to unforgiveness and bitterness. It also helps others sins to be covered. *Above all keep your love for one another fervent, because love covers a multitude of sins. Show hospitality to one another without complaining (1 Peter 4:8-9 NET).* There it is again… above all keep love, or the greatest is love.

God is trying to show us something here. He is telling us that when we love with all our hearts much good comes out of it. How can you love if you cannot forgive? How can you love if you do not love from the heart of Jesus? It is impossible to know how to really love, if you do not know the one who Himself *is* love and it is also impossible to show love if you do not comprehend that you have also had to be forgiven time and time again.

Our Father in Heaven always looks at the heart. He does not equate us to our past mistakes. He does not hold us hostage for something we truly repented for. He is a good Father. He also is a just and righteous judge.

But the LORD said unto Samuel, look not on his countenance, or on the height of his stature; because I have refused him: for the LORD seeth not as man seeth; for man looketh on the outward appearance, but the LORD looketh on the heart (1 Samuel 16:7 KJV). We see through the lens of our mortal beings, but God sees through the lens of truth. Appearances can be deceiving, and truth can be hidden in plain sight. Therefore, we must have discernment from the Lord to know what is really going on. We as well must have His heart to know the truth, for He is the truth. Many times, we are judging someone's outward appearance, when we should be checking their inward motives. The truth will set us all free, if we let it.

Secondly, let us deal with the how can you love if you won't forgive portion. Do you really think it is possible to say you love someone if forgiveness is not something you are able to do? I can answer that with a resounding NO for you. It is possible that you believe that you can love and that you are loving people. Yet, I will be honest with you that love is a poisonous kind of love. And that poisonous love hurts not only the other person but you yourself also.

Have you ever heard the story of The Scorpion and the Frog? It is an animal fable who's first origins were found in the 1933 Russian novel, "The German Quarter": by Lev Nitoburg. This fable is very powerful. It shows us the truth that we may not want to sometimes admit. It goes something like this…

A scorpion wants to cross a river but cannot swim, so it asks a frog to carry it across. The frog hesitates, afraid that the scorpion might sting it, but the scorpion promises not to, pointing out that it would drown if it killed the frog in the middle of the river. The frog considers this argument sensible and agrees to transport the scorpion. Midway across the river, the scorpion stings the frog anyway, dooming them both. The dying frog asks the scorpion why it stung despite knowing the consequence, to which the scorpion replies: "I am sorry, but I couldn't resist the urge. It's in my nature."

There you have it. Our intentions may be to love despite unforgiveness but unforgiveness will have us holding grudges and taking up offenses for the little things, the unknown things, and the things we simply created in our own minds. Without getting healing and deliverance from this spirit it will just lay dormant inside of you. There it is waiting for an opportune time

Unforgiveness and Bitterness

to cause you to not be able to resist its nasty bite. That is unforgiveness's nature my friends and it drowns both parties.

Unforgiveness leaves room for so many things to manifest negatively. Some of these things are anger, hostility, haughty imaginations, grudges, bitterness, offense, and eventually hate. For these very reasons you must find liberation. You cannot say you love when unforgiveness is clouding your heart. Love should always be unconditional and not based on how we see fit to love someone.

Did you know that God has forgiven you of so much? Not just the one time when He took on all our iniquities, but still to this day He is forgiving you of your wrong doings. His love for you has always and will always be unconditional. Yet, how dare you say you have a right to not forgive, when He has never withheld forgiveness from you. Friends, we got to do better.

Thirdly, are you ready to forgive? How bad do you want it? If you are not ready to forgive, it will all be done in vain and since God knows our hearts, He will know your true condition. We cannot fool Him, so be sure you are ready to surrender to forgiveness. Be ready for love for real.

In forgiving someone else it is twofold. Because in forgiving a person you are also subconsciously saying that you are going to forgive yourself as well.

The Silent Killer

We cannot outright say "I forgive them", without outright saying "Lord, forgive me too." Sorry, it just does not work that way. Forgiveness is a two-way street.

Look at the Lord's prayer. When the disciples asked Jesus to teach them how to pray. He said pray in this manner. What He did was give them a blueprint for prayer. We cannot now stray from it, as if we know a better way.

Check this part out. *And forgive us our debts, as we forgive our debtors (Matthew 6:12 KJV)*. This is saying… forgive me of my sin, as I am forgiving those who sinned against me. We cannot say we are forgiven, when we do not forgive others. We also cannot forgive others without first admitting that we too need forgiveness and repenting for our wrong doings.

Being the one to try and hold debts over other people's heads, without considering our own debts leaves us to ensue the wrath and judgement of our creator. As I told you earlier, God is a righteous and just judge. He is fair and will forgive us for much. Yet, if we cannot extend forgiveness, He as well does observe that behavior. Next, we are going to look at this Biblically.

Let us read The Parable of the Unforgiving Servant. *Therefore is the kingdom of heaven likened unto a certain king, which would take account of his servants. And when he had begun to reckon, one was brought unto him, which owed him ten thousand talents (this would be considered millions of dollars today). But forasmuch as he had not to pay, his lord commanded him to be sold, and his wife, and children, and all that he had, and payment to be made. The servant therefore fell down, and worshipped him, saying, Lord, have patience with me, and I will pay thee all. Then the lord of that servant was moved with compassion, and loosed him, and forgave him the debt.*

But the same servant went out, and found one of his felowservants, which owed him an hundred pence: and he laid hands on him, and took him by the throat, saying, Pay me that thou owest. And his fellowservant fell down at his feet, and besought him, saying, Have patience with me, and I will pay thee all. And he would not: but went and cast him into prison, till he should pay the debt. So when his fellowservants saw what was done, they were very sorry, and came and told unto their lord all that was done. Then his lord, after that he had called him, said unto him, O thou wicked servant, I forgave thee all that debt, because thou desiredst me: shouldest not thou also have had compassion on thy fellowservant, even as I had pity on thee? And his lord was wroth, and delivered him to the tormentors, till he should pay all that was due unto him. So likewise shall my heavenly Father do also unto you, if ye from your hearts forgive not everyone his brother their trespasses (Matthew 18:23-35 KJV).

Here you see the parable told to Peter by Jesus. The picture painted is quite clear right? You cannot ask God to forgive you of debts that you owe, He forgive you and then you hold the right to not forgive someone of the debt they owe you. It just does not work like that in the Kingdom of God. Once your sins are pardoned, your heart should be moved to pardon others who might have hurt you.

Forgiveness is not so much for the other person as much as it is for you. Forgiveness's beautiful nature is so freeing. It so easily releases you of turmoil and pain. It breaks the cage and allows you to finally fly free. Forgiveness has the word *give* in it, because it gives you so much life, love, freedom, and happiness.

Prayer

Father God,

I understand better than I ever have, how important forgiveness is. I am so sorry for my unforgiveness. I ask that You release me from this prison. I do not want to not love correctly. I need Your assistance with this thing.

I repent for all the times I have held grudges. I release those hatreds right now. I forgive (name the people) who hurt me. I give them to You Lord, and I let go of the hurt, the strife, and the hatred. I also ask that You forgive me for those whom I have hurt. There is no place I want to leave uncovered. I choose to be free in You.

Thank You for forgiving me time and time again. You are so kind and such a good Father. I love You so much. I do not deserve Your love, but I am ever so grateful that You give it freely and unconditionally. In Jesus's name I pray, Amen.

Chapter 7

Pride and Deception

These two spirits are a favorite snare of the enemy. He loves to pass these two out because he deals strongly with them himself. Pride is his signature and deception is his comfort. He finds reassurance and rest in these two disgusting characteristics of his. We are going to help you not do the same today.

Satan dealt heavy with pride from the beginning of his creation as Lucifer. The Bible says in Ezekiel 28 that he was full of wisdom and perfect in beauty. He was created with every precious stone and gem and his settings were made of gold. He was set as a covering of God's glory. Lucifer was made as a guardian cherub.

Lucifer was once blameless in his behavior from the day of his creation until something changed. What changed? Because of his being full of wisdom and his beauty being perfect he changed his thought of himself. Instead of seeing God as magnificent for creating him so incredibly, he thought of himself as the most magnificent. He became proud and thought of himself higher than he should have.

Pride and Deception

This pride caused him to sin against God. He became violent in his pursuit to outrank God. The very one who created him, who loved him, and there Lucifer only felt competition with Him. It is crazy how fast pride can cause one to sin. Once that spirit bites you, you become infected.

This is the way of pride. It gives you a puffed-up sense of who you are and what you carry. It makes you regard your gift as "greater than". Pride eats character up and leaves you open to satan's devices. It is a serious thing that causes serious offense.

Pride likes to link up with offense, lies, delusion, deception, false humility, and comparison to name a few. It is a messy little fox, that destroys every vine it eats from. Spoiling your fruit and leaving your soul to harden and rot. Pride once it enters you, moves fast like cancer and leaves your head spinning. It is one ride you do not want to take.

The enemy is still full of pride, that is how destructive pride really is. It leads you down the path of no return. It prevents you from even thinking you need help. This is another reason it is so hard to get free from it. Because you are legit thinking you are okay and are functioning as your best.

Satan is also a master at deception. Deception is the number one tool in his ammunition used against us. He pulls this bad boy out and aims it with precision. He knows what he is doing, but he also knows that most times we have no clue what he is doing. We fall privy to his devices, because we are clueless to how he moves.

I want to talk about his deception for a minute. He used this line of defense against Eve in the garden of Eden. How was he able to pull this off you may be wondering? Well, first he is a master manipulator and I talked about it in chapter five. Second, he is a great chameleon. The Bible says that satan disguises himself as an angel of light (2 Corinthians 11:14).

Okay, now we will go back to when satan deceived Eve. Eve was the first woman created; she was created from Adam's rib. Made in splendor and beauty and both Adam and Eve were made in God's image and likeness. Now remember from up above that pride is what messed up satan in the first place, because his beauty and splendor got the best of him and made him not only compare but think of himself higher than God. This behavior got him thrown out of Heaven. Are you even the least bit surprised that he would then become jealous and angry that God decided to create us in His own image and likeness? I know that stung satan to his rotten core and of course he would set out to try and destroy us.

How would he attempt to do that? What would be his first line of attack? To somehow deceive us into believing the same lie he created within himself. Which is that we could be equal to or better than God. Crazy that it worked and still is working on so many still today.

Now, remember satan is not an idiot. The Bible told us he was full of wisdom, it never said anywhere that God stripped him of the things He created him with. As you just read in 2 Corinthians he is still coming to people as an angel of light, meaning he comes looking as beautiful as he was once created to be. So, I am positive he plotted and schemed. He watched and looked for the crack in the door that he could squeeze in through.

He found what he was looking for in Eve. Now, I do not know truly what he found that led him to know that he could deceive her, but I can make an educated guess. Satan's tricks are always the same, they may look different, but generations repeat the iniquities of their forefathers most often. So, because of this understanding on curses, I see many women struggle with murmuring, complaining, back biting, and unstable emotions. This leads me to speculate that maybe, just maybe he overheard her on a bad day or two. She was upset and said something that left the impression that she was unhappy at that moment or frustrated in some way and he took the opportunity to slide in as a friendly face.

He appeared in the form of a serpent (a snake). Snakes are very sneaky and can appear without you even noticing they are there until they are already upon you. Even that should have been a red flag of some sort because what in the world are you doing sneaking up on someone? The Bible even says in Genesis 3:1 that the serpent was more subtil or we could say craftier than any other animal in the field. He knew what he was doing from the beginning and as usual satan banks on us being ignorant of his devices. Unfortunately, as I stated earlier, we normally are.

So, he watches from afar until his opportune time. He may have even warmed her up a bit with hellos, hand waves, and head bobs. Who knows what he did, but he is a master at deception, so I am sure he warmed her up some way, somehow. I know he was looking forward to the day that would eventually come. Finally, it was time to strike, and he did so with so much skill.

Check out his approach. *And he said unto the woman, Yea, hath God said, Ye shall not eat of every tree of the garden? And the woman said unto the serpent, We may eat of the fruit of the trees of the garden: but of the fruit of the tree which is in the midst of the garden, God hath said, Ye shall not eat of it, neither shall ye touch it, lest ye die. And the serpent said unto the woman, Ye shall not surely die: for God doth know that in the day ye eat thereof, then your eyes shall be opened, and ye shall be as gods, knowing good and evil. And when the woman saw that the tree was good for food, and that it was pleasant to the eyes, and a tree to be desired to make one wise, she*

took of the fruit thereof, and did eat, and gave also unto her husband with her; and he did eat (Genesis 3: 1-6 KJV).

Do you see how skillful he was with his words? He changed things only slightly enough to make her perceive it just a bit differently. He knew what God had told them, he wanted her to say it, so he could get her to see it from her own point of view. It is a masterful tactic in manipulation. Make you see it from your own words and then twist them ever so much, until I get you hook, line and sinker.

So, as you see he asked her *did God say* you cannot eat of *every* tree of the garden? The key words here are did God say and every. He can easily hear and when God told them they could eat of every tree except the one in the middle, satan new that was the golden ticket. So, he asks her a rhetorical question basically. Then she answers as God told them and what does satan say? You will surely not die. Here we see direct rebellion against what the Lord said.

As if that was not enough, he goes on and adds fuel to the lie he told. He says God knows that once you eat it, your eyes shall open, and you will be as a god knowing good and evil. That was the draw right there. You will become like God and become wiser. Boom… Got her… Hook, line, and sinker.

Next, we see that once he said that, that Eve received what he said because the Bible goes on to say that when Eve saw that the tree was good for food,

The Silent Killer

pleasant to the eyes, and a tree to be desired to make you wise, that she took the fruit and ate it. Here we see what I talked about in chapter five. Satan presents things by the lust of the flesh, the lust of the eyes, and the pride of life. Here he presented all three of them to Eve.

He repeats things, like I said… never anything new, but mastering what he always does, and for this reason Paul tells us in the Bible not to be ignorant to satan's devices. Same dirty dog with the same dirty tricks, but you better let that silly dog know that tricks are for kids. You are gaining wisdom and understanding in the spirit and will not keep falling prey to the enemy. The more you learn the truth of God's word, the more you become equipped to fight back. Jesus only used the word against satan when he came to tempt Him and you can do the same, but you must study.

What satan did here was use deception against Eve. This great deception caused man to fall. This brought sin into a place that only knew holiness. After the fall of man, we now are born into sin because satan tainted the perfection of God's creation. This was his goal all along. And though he met that goal, today it is still his goal, and he roams the earth looking for whom he can devour (1 Peter 5:8).

We are in a time where satan wants to prevent and pervert the glory just like he once did. Now he does this through pride and deception that has

Pride and Deception

brought about offense. It is not good enough to just draw you into pride, or seduce you through deception, but now he is adding offense into the mix of this already deadly brew. It is sad to see so many saints fall into this trap. Let's take a moment to see how offense is introduced through these two spirits.

Pride is easily able to mask the true conditions of one's inner man and heart. The Bible tells us this… *The heart is deceitful above all things, and desperately wicked: who can know it? The LORD search the heart… (Jeremiah 17:9-10 KJV).* Here we see that our heart can be not only deceitful but also very wicked and we may not even know it. Yet, God will, because He always searches the heart.

Pride traps you inside your own deception of the opinion you hold of yourself and/or your importance. Once it encages you, you then have put bars up around yourself. Now with the barriers or walls you have built it is hard for truth to infiltrate and set you free. This is why pride and deception are so bad. They are like self-inflicted traps set by satan but administered by you, so it is that much harder to get free because you believe within your own mind that you are okay and are already free.

Here is a scripture that will paint this picture perfectly for you. *A brother offended is harder to be won than a strong city… (Proverbs 18:19 KJV).* So, here we see that it is easier to win a fortified city with the strongest walls enclosing it, than it is to get through the walls of offense that someone built around their heart. That is crazy to even try to believe, but sadly it is true. I know that this is a fact because pride and deception obscure the truth in a way that someone would have to get you to trust what they are pointing out over what you yourself actually believe.

That is not an easy thing to do at all. When you have a certain thought in your head, or are conditioned to believe something, it is nearly impossible to cause you to see it another way. Usually, it takes years or you yourself finally being fed up with the results you are getting for you to be freed from that deception. It is also very hard with pride because many must fall to finally get the picture that they were blinded by their own ignorance. The good news is you can become free, but it is all up to you.

Prayer

Lord,

Here I am before You once again. I know that I need to be set free from pride and deception. I do not want to be held any longer by these two things. This is not the life I want for myself at all. I ask You to set me free today.

I repent right now for allowing pride to set in. I as well repent for allowing satan to deceive me with his wicked deception. I am decreeing right now that I will no longer allow myself to be ignorant to satan's devices. I am a child of God and I see truth from Your eyes oh Lord. I am free from this bondage right now in Jesus's name.

Thank You for forgiveness. I am grateful for a brand-new day. I thank You for opening my eyes today. I do not take any of this for granted. In Jesus's name I pray, Amen.

Chapter 8

Immaturity and Rejection

We have reached our final chapter. I do want you to know that none of these spirits are in any kind of order or hierarchy. I just wanted to write on what God highlighted to me in my spirit. There are tons more that we could have put in here and if there are any that you know of that I forgot, please be sure to call those out in your prayer time as well. This freedom is for you, so go ahead and get completely free. There is no point in getting partial deliverance. I want you totally free.

Immaturity and rejection are some jerk devils lol. I am being funny in the sense that they are all extremely horrible in their own functions. Yet, I will say that I have seen these two spirits ruin some of the greatest people that seem to have the most potential. I have no proof of this, but as I have watched these spirits at work, it's like they attack this exact kind of person. The one who is called to be the greatest or who would impact the world in some earth-shaking way.

Immaturity and Rejection

Immaturity is defined as: *Behavior that is appropriate to someone younger.* A person who is a child will likely be childish, but a grown up should act fully grown. Yet so many times I see the exact opposite of both of those things happening. I know children and teenagers who are more mature than some of these adults. It is a sad reality, but nevertheless I see it happen quite often.

The Bible even talks about this. ***My friends, stop thinking like children. Think like mature people and be as innocent as tiny babies (1 Corinthians 14:20 CEV).*** I have heard the saying that "Innocence is inversely proportional to maturity". This is basically saying that as life moves forward you go through different experiences which mature you and take away your innocence.

Yet, we see the complete opposite in the scripture I just quoted. They are not supposed to replace one another, but they are supposed to be parallel with one another. Maturity and innocence can be lived out at the same time. Life experiences should not make you jaded to the point that you lose your innocence and wonder. You can be mature and full of wonder, just as you can be childlike in your faith, and mature in your character at the same time.

Verily I say unto you, Except ye be converted, and become as little children, ye shall not enter into the kingdom of heaven (Matthew 18:3 KJV). What is Jesus

The Silent Killer

saying here? He is showing us that children have such an amazing faith. You cannot shake a child's faith when they believe in something. Without this child-like faith, we cannot enter the Kingdom of Heaven.

For example, my son Chase had been praying for like six months straight that God would give him a baby brother. It had been literally every night consistently; it was the same prayer too. "God, please give me a baby brother because there are too many sisters in here." I felt so bad because my husband and I were done. We already had four kids and I just could not handle pregnancy again, plus our son Chase is seven years old, we did not want to start all over again.

Well, that was what we thought, God obviously had other plans. The Bible tells us that the prayers of the righteous availeth much and it never said kids could not be in that number. The Lord answered my son's prayer, and I became pregnant. Here is the kicker, I was so nervous that we would end up having another girl because we have three girls and just one son, so I knew that it was a high chance we could have another little girl. My husband and I got to the point when we could find out the sex of the baby and the morning of, I was kind of nervous.

My son Chase comes in and says "Mommy, you do not need to be nervous, God told me from the beginning that it would be a boy. Why would God only answer my prayer halfway, I asked Him to give us a baby, so why would it not be a brother? I asked God for a baby brother, so don't worry, it will be a boy." The level of confidence my son said it with blew my mind and actually calmed me down immediately. We went to the appointment and of course we are having a baby boy. That was absolute faith my son spoke in. Like I wrote earlier, childlike faith just cannot be shaken.

Immaturity or childishness is not the same as childlikeness. Being childlike is speaking of the positive qualities that children tend to have like innocence, vulnerability, wonder, hope, glee, unguardedness, and love. We as adults can learn from those qualities. When someone says "You are childish" they are usually referring to negative qualities like being immature, erratic, unpredictable, irresponsible, and foolish. These are not good qualities to have when you are an adult but are more expected or understood to happen in children, which is why it is called being childish.

Here is what the Bible says concerning this matter. ***When I was a child, I spake as a child, I understood as a child, I thought as a child: but when I became a man, I put away childish things (1 Corinthians 13:11 KJV).*** So, as I stated, it is expected for children to be childish, but not so much when you become an adult. At that point you should be putting those childish things away. You should now speak, understand, and reason as an adult.

The Silent Killer

Okay, let me move on to rejection. This is another one that goes hand and hand with being immature. I will talk a little bit about this spirit and then bring them together. The more you know, the more you can get free. Here we go!

Reject is defined as: *To refuse to accept, consider, submit to, take for some purpose, or use*. Rejection is one that causes long-term effects if not dealt with swiftly. When you feel you are refused it is a blow to your ego. It hurts to be turned down. Rejection will magnify that hurt and twist the truth.

Rejection leaves you hurt and broken to the point that you end up rejecting yourself. It is the spirit's main aim. If it can get you to reject yourself, it will not matter what anyone else says or does, because you already wrote yourself off. Rejection is sly with how it enters, but once in there it devours you slowly but purposefully. Its purpose being to make you lose all hope and to utterly stop your belief.

Hope and belief are very powerful things. When someone has hope, it makes them believe that they have purpose. They see the brighter side of things; they know that tomorrow is just one day away. Hope washes away pessimism and exchanges it for optimism. And when someone is optimistic, nothing can ever hold them back from reaching their goals. This is what rejection wants to kill within you. This spirit wants you to have zero hope for the future and to never reach any of your goals.

Immaturity and Rejection

Rejection was at the core of the fall of man. This was brought into play when man rejected God and His command and chose evil over good. It is still at the core of all we do. The question has always been, will we keep rejecting God or will we believe what He says? This is even the case in self-rejection.

God said that we are a good creation and when we allow rejection in, we stop believing that very thing. Check this out. In the very beginning God created everything out of Him, we came out of His glory. After He created everything, He was thoroughly pleased with His work. ***And God saw everything that he had made, and behold, it was very good (Genesis 1:31 KJV).*** Everything includes us, my friends.

When we reject ourselves as good and replace what God said with what the enemy has put before us to believe, we are rejecting God. Through that behavior we are saying we doubt God's ability, His sovereign word, and are calling Him a liar. We are now once again taking satan at his word and rejecting our Savior. That is never okay. When will we stop agreeing with dysfunction?

We will stop rejecting what God says, when we receive it with gladness. ***For everything created by God is good, and nothing is to be rejected if it is received with thanksgiving, for it is made holy by the word of God and prayer (1 Timothy 4:4 ESV).*** This is the truth plain and simple. But we cannot see the truth of God because

The Silent Killer

we are ungrateful and full of negativity. Our thoughts hold to the bad before they believe in the good.

Psychologists call this thinking "negative bias". They say the human brain has a natural tendency to give weight to and remember negative experiences more than positive ones. It is said our brains are wired that way. I honestly do not agree. We do not have to be susceptible to thinking this way.

I truly believe that this way of thinking came about with the fall of man. When sin entered the equation, everything equals out to the sum of the evil that was performed at that time. When we become born again, we become born of the bloodline of Christ. This in turn makes us no longer hold on to the old pattern of living. We become free of the curse of being born into sin and shaped by iniquity.

Since rejection has been around since the fall of man, we are a lot more able to fall into that trap. Once again, you must go back in the book and recall my telling you that the devil is a one-trick pony. He does not usually come up with a new battle plan. He uses what worked before and just repackages it in the way that will suit you best. We love what sparkles and shines, but how many know that everything that glitters does not mean it is gold?

Rejection does not have to become you. You do not have to accept the plan of the enemy. There is no reason that your life should not be lived to the fullness

Immaturity and Rejection

that God designed for it to be lived. If His word says that He came to give you life and life more abundantly, then believe that. It is the very law within our Father, that His word does not return to Him void. He will not ever lie to you, and He is not a man that He ever could.

How do these two spirits cause offense? They easily change and or shape your mentality towards yourself and others. When your mindset is skewed in any way it causes you to look out with 3D glasses on. By that I mean it makes everything jump out that is not even needing to be magnified and is truly just a figment of your imagination and the way your viewpoint is set up at that current time. Your glasses may need glasses because you are seeing all wrong.

Immaturity can easily be replaced by maturation. Rejection can also be rejected with ease, when you decide to choose acceptance. Both are non-factors; they are simply a choice. We choose what we will or won't become. I say it is time to choose growth and it is high time we choose loving ourselves. How can we help anyone else grow or anyone else heal, if we do not first help ourselves? Love is a beautiful thing, and its beauty shines the brightest when it is reflected out of us from the light of Abba Father.

Joy is contagious! Happiness is motivating! And love, well, love is a recipe that changes and heals disaster and heartache! Let's start right here with these three things. For it is beyond time that we let offense go.

We do not have to be people who are easily offended. There is so much more to life than becoming stuck in this foolishness. It zaps joy, dissolves happiness, and takes love completely off the table. Who wants to live in such darkness? There is so much more to life, there is much more in love, there is so much more to learn and see when we become unoffendable.

Prayer

Father,

I receive all this. I am here and I am standing in need of change. I really want to be free. Free from every spirit that is holding me back from fully living. Today is my day.

I am not going to get up from this place until I know that I am fully free. I will stay here all night! I will pursue You until! There is nothing more important to me than You. Here in Your presence is where I long to be.

Immaturity and rejection cannot have me. I will not let up. I have been plagued by these spirits long enough. Now, I am breaking out of their hold and running to impact the world with the name of Jesus. I am changing so I can help others change.

Freedom is a choice and choose freedom. I choose liberation today and every day here after. I will walk this thing out. Offense you are no longer my portion. I evict you today.

I repent right now for embracing offense. I repent Lord for allowing it to be my comfort and my hiding place. I now run to You, for You are my strong tower. You are my line of defense. I love You and renounce everything connected to the demon called offense. I am free now in Jesus's name, Amen.

Conclusion

Offense is a steppingstone to destruction. The Bible says in John *The thief cometh not, but for to steal, and to kill, and to destroy... (John 10:10 KJV).* Offense is the very bait he uses to destroy you spiritually, mentally, emotionally, and physically. This is why I called it the silent killer, because it hits you on every level. Wake up my friends and move past offenses quickly. I hope this book assists you in becoming free.

I remember when God decided to show me Hell. He said He will take me through it slowly over time, but something that stood out and shook me to my core from the part I have seen is this. I was in a very dim hallway and there was this room with a big black chamber door. On the door was written… The Heart Chamber. I felt led to open the door.

As I entered the room, it was as well very dimly lit in there. Right directly in the middle of the room was this humongous heart. I felt the hate and the offense that oozed out of that heart. You could smell the unforgiveness, the insecurity, the full-on negativity that was dwelling inside that black organ. It was heartbreaking truly.

Conclusion

I looked closely and the heart was black and no longer beating. It was covered in ivy and the ivy was choking the life out of that heart. I inquired the Lord about it. I said "Father, what is going on here?" He responded... "Daughter, that is what offense does to your heart." I was appalled and very hurt, because I know many who cannot move past offenses. To imagine their hearts looking like that heart was deeply troubling for me.

Ivy is a suffocating agent. When it grows on houses, it literally suffocates or chokes out the beauty of the structure. It will eventually disrupt the foundation of the house. Which causes things to shift and cracks to then form within the walls and through the grounds of the home. Is this something you want happening within your heart?

If you notice on the front cover of my book there you will see a heart covered with green ivy. The heart is still red, but there are black spots upon it. This is a heart that is dealing with offense, it is still beating, but the ivy is slowly doing its job. It is killing the heart. Do not allow offense to do this to your heart slowly too. Make it your business to get truly delivered. You deserve to live in total freedom, so happy liberation day!

A Call to Repentance

Did you know that holding offense is unacceptable to God? The Bible tells us… *You shall not take vengeance or bear a grudge against the sons of your own people, but you shall love your neighbor as yourself: I am the LORD (Leviticus 19:18 ESV).* What this means is we should not hold offenses against our own people but should allow them the same opportunity to receive the love you give yourself. What right do we have to not give of ourselves, when God has so graciously given of Himself repeatedly? We must take a deeper look at what we say is alright in the eyes of Abba Father.

If we remain nonchalant in our willingness to let go of offense, where will that get us? Trough stagnation or straight refusal to let these issues go we can easily become complacent in our pursuit of God. Without forgiveness, we can gain a tainted lens regarding our Father. And sadly, without the right view of Abba we will lack compassion, hope, and strength as individuals and as a nation. We must get back to the understanding that offense is a huge hinderance in our walk with God.

If you know that you have been lacking in desire to get over offenses. If you have been having a hard time in your relationship with the Lord. Trust me, it is okay. The reason that it is alright is because the God of second chances is here to give you a fresh start. Repeat after me…

"Father, I know that I have broken your laws and my sins have separated me from you. I am truly sorry, and now I want to turn from my sinful ways toward you. Lord, please forgive me, and help me to be guided away from sin. I believe that your son, Jesus Christ died on the cross for me, was resurrected from the dead, and is alive today. I invite Jesus to become the Lord of my life, to rule in my heart this day forward. I ask that you send your Holy Spirit to help me. In Jesus name, Amen."

If you just prayed that prayer with me, you have been made brand new. You must steward this new life and guard your heart with all diligence. I would advise you to find a church where you can be with like-minded believers that will help you grow in Christ. Talk to them about being baptized, it is necessary, and God ask that we do this. Remember to pray and study your word, this will sharpen you in the things of the spirit. I love you with the love of the Lord and welcome to the family.

About the Author

Emily Strickland is a dynamic and humble woman after God's own heart. She is a wife and mother, and she believes very strongly that her family is her first ministry. Emily began serving Jesus fully and totally at age twenty-four. She was radically changed after finding Jesus Christ. Since that experience, she carries a holy fire, and a need to bring revival to the world. Emily operates under the power of the Holy Spirit; she ministers strongly in healing and deliverance. God has called her as a mouthpiece to this generation.

Emily is an example of God's power being able to transform anyone's life. She is a voice of healing to women who have gone through traumatic experiences. Her goal is to uplift and empower people through the word of God, and see their lives forever changed. She alongside her husband Chazdon Strickland are the founders of Ignite the Globe. They have four children and are currently residing in Florida.

If you would like to reach out to her, you can email her at redeemedvoicepublishing@yahoo.com

Also, you can find her on Facebook under Emily Strickland Ministries.

About the Author

Be sure to join her page Inspired and Brave also on the Facebook platform. There she puts up encouraging post and videos to help women to become inspired by other women and brave enough to fight for their dreams.

Please follow her blog Moments of Motivation and check out her courses, other books, and many other resources at Emilykstrickland.com

Made in the USA
Columbia, SC
06 June 2025